Institute of Education
University of London

Communication skills and the knowledge economy: language, literacy and the production of meaning

FIONA DOLOUGHAN

© Institute of Education 2001

Institute of Education University of London
20 Bedford Way
London WC1H 0AL

Pursuing Excellence in Education

British Library Cataloguing in Publication Data:
A catalogue record for this publication is
available from the British Library

ISBN 0-85473-643-3

Dedication
To my maternal grandfather, Robert
Gordon, whose eternal optimism despite
difficult circumstances still inspires me
today and to Margaret Doloughan, my
paternal grandmother, who faced every
challenge in a spirit of kindness and
generosity.

Produced in Great Britain by
Reprographic Service
Institute of Education University of London

Printed by Formara Limited
16 The Candlemakers,
Temple Farm Industrial Estate,
Southend on Sea, Essex SS2 5RX

CONTENTS

ACKNOWLEDGEMENTS

I am particularly grateful to Geoff Whitty, who, as Dean of Research, first suggested I put together a proposal for the *Perspectives on Education Policy* series and to Sally Power, whose constructive criticisms of my drafts encouraged and motivated me. Thanks, too, to Mary and Nick, my colleagues in the Academic Literacies team; and to CCS for providing an intellectually stimulating environment. Last, but not least, to Deborah, Brigid and Sally in the Publications Office, for in the first instance waiting patiently for my manuscript and then preparing it for publication with great care and attention to detail.

discourse. I shall review in particular some of the issues relating to communication skills and their importance in the construction of the knowledge economy. I shall then problematise notions of communication in relation to 'theories' of language, learning and the production of meaning which challenge some of the assumptions on which the skills model is based. Finally I reflect on the implications of these theories for the learning and teaching process and the acquisition of language and literacy.

HIGHER EDUCATION TODAY

In a recent profile in the Education section of *The Independent* (7 September 2000), Edward de Bono, in conversation with Anthea Milnes, talked about his career, interests and ideas. In the context of publication of his new book, *The De Bono Code Book*, which 'tackles the subject of language and how it limits our perceptions and communication', he refers to the education system in the UK, which he characterises as 'self-satisfied and change-resistant' (Milnes 2000: 10). Comparing the business sector to the academic and political domains, he concludes that 'of all sectors in society, business is the most interested in thinking'. Later in the article he asserts: 'So much thinking in universities looks backwards ... you can analyse the past, but you have to design the future'.

I have chosen to relate the contents of this interview with de Bono for a number of reasons. First, while articulating the tension that exists between the business world and the academy, de Bono embodies (the possibility of) a successful alliance between otherwise differing domains. Second, he flags up some of the pertinent and inter-related issues with which this publication is concerned, namely the role of language in the communicative process; the relationship between language and thought; and the tensions that exist between the various stakeholders competing to design and direct the future of society.

1
HE and the production of 'useful' knowledge: designing the future

INTRODUCTION

It would be difficult to deny that the HE (higher education) system in Britain today has come under considerable pressure to adapt to the perceived needs and imperatives of the new (world) economic and social orders of the twenty-first century. Issues of funding and accountability, of social and educational mission, of levels and modes of participation and of the management of (limited) resources constitute some of the parameters of the debates surrounding the nature of the compact between HE and society.

In this book I shall examine critically the nature of this compact as articulated in the Dearing Report and suggest an alternative reading that highlights the ambiguities, tensions and anxieties disclosed by the

FOREWORD

What is education for? What can society expect from its universities? What kind of human being do we envisage as the product of the (higher) education system? And do we need, in any case, a fundamental rethinking of what education could be and needs to be as we move further into 'the knowledge economy'?

These are some of the questions tackled in this book. Taking the Dearing Committee report on *Higher Education in the Learning Society* as a point of departure, that broad set of questions is debated around the specific focus of communication skills and the knowledge economy. The deep contradictions at the core of the current public debate on education are identified: the profession of a concern with the future – the by now ritualistic invocation of new trinities 'flexibility', 'adaptability', 'creativity' – on the one hand and the intense anxieties leading to backward-looking education practices and curricula on the other. Beyond such contradictions lie others: between skills, usefulness and employability, and wisdom, breadth and deeper understanding.

Fiona Doloughan's analysis remains calm and measured; she understands that the contemporary period does not lend itself to easy, clear solutions. Yet the book is not content with critique. It shows us trends in newer forms of communication, and from these develops a sense of achievable and productive goals for education, a sense of how humans could act productively in that unstable world. Beyond showing the challenges, the book points to possible ways forward.

GUNTHER KRESS
Professor of English/Education,
Institute of Education

Third, his view of analysis as being essentially retrospective, while the concept of design, as he sees it, relates to the future echoes Gunther Kress's contention (Kress 2000b) that critique is a necessary but insufficient condition for constructing a social future in a fast-changing world. 'While critique', Kress writes, 'looks at the present through the means of past production, Design shapes the future through deliberate deployment of representational resources in the designer's interest' (Kress 2000b: 160).

I shall be returning to Kress's notion of representational resources shortly but for now, by way of introduction, it is sufficient to see in de Bono's remarks a concern with the inability or unwillingness of our education system as currently constituted to cope with the challenges of a new era and its failure to exploit the productive potentialities offered by thinking in unaccustomed and unconventional ways. Of course de Bono's views cannot go unanalysed; he, like others, has a particular interest in promoting such concepts. Nevertheless, given the seriousness of the charges which he levels against education and the fact that his concerns are neither unique nor totally without justification, it is necessary not simply to write them off but to see them as representative of voices or (constructed) cultural positions with a stake in a particular vision of the future.

A VISION FOR THE FUTURE: THE DEARING REPORT

It was, precisely, concern with the future of HE in the UK that prompted the gathering of information, evidence, ideas and opinions by the members of the Dearing Committee, a process which led to the publication in 1997 of their report, *Higher Education in the Learning Society*. This outlined a vision for education over the next 20 years in the context of a rapidly changing society. Indeed some of the considerations taken into account by the committee mirror de Bono's concerns about the value(s) of an education system which is failing to prepare a sufficient number of individuals for participation in the social and economic life of the country. Against the backdrop of expansion in HE and the political, economic and social pressures being exerted on HEIs (higher education institutions), the Dearing Report sets out to examine the (changing) nature of the 'compact between higher education and society' (1.27) and to suggest possible ways forward given the competing claims of academics, politicians, economists and consumers, both potential and actual, of HE. While recognising that in absolute terms the future is unknowable, the report nevertheless depicts a future society in which the ability of individuals to manage change in line with technological and social developments will be crucial as will be their willingness to be 'creative', 'resourceful' and 'flexible'. There will be on the part of individuals a 'requirement to renew, update and widen their knowledge and skills throughout life' (1.16). They will also need to be able to transfer skills from one domain to another (cf. 3.5) and to react to diverse and changing circumstances (cf. 4.20). 'To survive in the labour market of the future', the report contends, 'workers will need new sets of skills, to work across conventional boundaries and see connections between processes, functions and disciplines and, in particular, to manage the learning which will support their careers' (4.21). The job of HE in such a context will be to 'equip graduates with the skills and attributes needed to be effective in a changing world of work and upon which to found and manage a number of careers' (4.22).

At one level such views seem entirely reasonable. It would be difficult to argue against the need to adapt to changing conditions or circumstances. From this perspective the Dearing Report has much to recommend it. It examines some of the contextual factors driving change and looks at the types of demands likely to be made on HEIs by various interested parties in the future. While conceding that nothing is certain, it suggests that an examination of the facts, figures and trends would justify a particular vision and course of action. Yet ultimately, I would contend, the language in which the report is couched and the assumptions on which it is constructed reveal an agenda that begs as many questions as it answers. By looking more closely and more critically at selected textual extracts, I would like to argue that the text is marked, at a lexical and structural level, by particular economic and political positions which are open to challenge. In addition, the apparently self-evident nature of the propositions, as well as the seemingly transparent language, becomes highly problematic on closer inspection.

THE DEARING REPORT: A CRITIQUE

The notion of accountability, a concept which has been imported from the fields of economics and accountancy and 'imposed' on education, rears its head early on in the report with respect to what society has a right to expect of HE: 'the community, as represented by the government, has a right to expect HE to be responsive to the developing needs of society' (1.9). This apparently benign claim raises all sorts of questions. Society, far from being monolithic, is in fact made up of different 'communities' or constituencies or interest groups. To which 'community' is the report referring: the 'community' of tax-payers perhaps? The phrase 'as represented by the government', which is grammatically linked by apposition to the preceding clause, suggests an uncritical view of the sometimes conflictual relationship between the representatives of government and the various constituencies which they may or may not in reality 'represent'. The expression 'to have a right to expect' someone to do something implies a rather moralistic view and relates back to the notion of accountability. Perhaps an ideology of 'rights and responsibilities' is being alluded to here. As for the 'developing needs of society', the open-endedness of the content of the proposition is belied by the preceding 'right to expect'. One tends to expect something solid, static, concrete rather than something that is potential or uncertain. The issue of what 'society' needs and who makes this kind of assessment is also open to question. There is an assumption here that the relationship between the participants mentioned in the sentence – community, government and society – is clear, when in fact it may well be problematic.

In fact, it seems to me that the tenor of the vision for the future lends too much weight to economic imperatives. While it would be naive to suggest that the notion of 'money making the world go round' has no currency in social reality, it is, I think, also fair to say that society's goals and individual aspirations may not always be reducible to 'bottom lines'. Yet the report speaks, for example, of the 'economic imperative ... to resume growth (1.15); of activities 'spurred by the demands of employers' (3.51); of the 'potential advantage in realising the mutual gain' for HE and the world of work (1.24); of a 'premium on knowledge' and a 'knowledge-based economy' (4.14), of educational targets (cf. 4.73), benchmarking (cf. 4.82), and the 'increasing emphasis on the role of HE in serving the needs of the economy' (4.78). I am not suggesting that one should simply dismiss these concepts and relationships because of the language in which they are couched. Rather I am pointing to the difficulties of engaging in debate where the terms of reference are treated as if they were neutral when in fact they are highly charged and are part of a political and economic context which also needs to be scrutinised.

Indeed the report itself betrays a Janus-like quality; it is underwritten by an essential ambiguity, which is reflected syntactically and at the level of propositional content, about the role of HE in relation to the world of work and a changing society. For example, while acknowledging that the authors of the report 'do not accept *a purely instrumental approach to HE* (the italics are mine), the text nevertheless continues: 'But higher education has become *central to the economic wellbeing of nations and individuals.* The qualities of mind that it develops will be the qualities that society increasingly needs to function efficiently' (4.2). This seems to be a case of putting the cart before the horse and begs a number of questions. In what way(s) has HE become central to the economic wellbeing of nations and individuals? The assumption seems to be that the role of education is to produce economically efficient and productive individuals. And what of the 'qualities of mind' that society (or rather individuals-in-society) needs to function effectively? Is HE already producing people with such qualities and needs only to expand and diversify its activities or does it need to change in line with economic imperatives? 'Above all', the report continues, 'the country must enable people, in large numbers and throughout life, to equip themselves for a world of work which is characterised by change' (4.2).

Elsewhere the report refers to the likelihood that in the future individuals will experience periods of employment, self-employment and unemployment. My question would be: are the qualities of mind needed to function effectively in the world of work the same qualities of mind required to endure periods of unemployment (or handle the challenges of self-employment)? I would suggest that the 'skills and attributes needed to be effective in a changing world of work' (4.22) may not necessarily be reducible to communication skills, numeracy and IT and indeed that attributes such as 'flexibility', 'adaptability', 'creativity' and 'ability to manage one's own learning' may or may not be sufficient for gaining fulfilment, depending both on what is meant by these terms and what individuals desire/value/are able to achieve within the social and economic framework that contains them. The whole question of the nature of the compact between individuals and the society of which they are a part (as opposed to that between HE and the world of work) remains unexamined. The implication is that individuals will be required to assume greater responsibility than in the past for their future prospects and prosperity. HE, it seems, must equip them so as to attain this goal. At the same time HE will increasingly be asked to assess the extent to which it is responding to the needs of employers. The potential for conflict of interest here is enormous. The question of whether individual and societal goals are ultimately compatible is one which raises itself, as does the issue of whether HE is to be driven by employment needs and/or is to respond to the needs of individual 'consumers': needs which may not always coincide.

To be fair, the report acknowledges the existence, if not the extent, of these tensions by making a number of concessions to what might otherwise be a rather too uncritical view of the world. While on the one hand remarking that the last 100 years or so has seen 'the transition to a society which is essentially scientifically and technologically based' (5.26), the report simultaneously refers to the crucial role to be played by research in the social sciences and humanities. In fact, it goes on to assert that the social sciences 'can help us to understand better the human aspects of changes in the world and how best to adapt to them' (5.30). What seems to underlie such a role for the social sciences (and indeed the humanities) is an implicit concern with the human 'fallout' from such a technologically and scientifically motivated future. There would appear to be a measure of anxiety about a future which fails to take account of 'the human aspects of change'. There is nothing intrinsically good (or bad) about change. It may or may not be welcome in a particular situation depending on who stands to benefit and to what extent. It may be that individuals and indeed whole societies need to adapt to changing circumstances and that such change needs to be managed. Ultimately change is motivated not just by economic, scientific and technological developments but by institutions, political parties and groups of people in whose interest it is to promote such change. Historical necessity and economic imperatives may be re-analysed and re-interpreted as a series of contingent interests and challengeable visions rather than as essential, teleological developments. Not only is the notion of change more problematic than it might at first appear but so too is that of adaptation. To adapt to one's situation may be positively or negatively construed depending on individual and societal circumstances. Adaptation may be a survival strategy or a coping mechanism rather than a resourceful deployment of energies and interests. It may lead to conformity and stasis rather than (r)evolutionary change.

Similar concerns come to the fore in a recent interview with Naomi Klein, Canadian author of an anti-corporate book, *No Logo* (2000), which argues that capitalism has become much more sophisticated, having co-opted alternative politics and culture, and that it is sometimes very difficult to see the power dynamics in society. There is the illusion of greater equality of opportunity and cultural homogeneity, while in fact society is becoming more fragmented and power and wealth are being concentrated into the hands of fewer and fewer people. In this brave new world corporations are more powerful than governments and global deregulation is simply the means to a corporate end. It seems to me that educational policies are in equal danger of being co-opted in the service of capitalism with the result that the potential of concepts like 'flexibility', 'adaptability' and 'creativity' are realised in actuality in rather an impoverished sense. Designing one's own future is a plausible option only for those who have the resources – technical, educational, financial and social. The politics of education are being masked by various competing agendas that need to be subjected to scrutiny, or what Klein calls 'radical critique'. There are real issues of access and equity (who will have the opportunity to attend HEIs or other sites of learning in the future); of curriculum design and delivery (what will be taught, by what means and by whom); of funding and accountability (who is to pay and what are they to expect in return); and of diversity and social representation (which kind of institutions will expect to accommodate which kind of people), issues which are contextually bound to social, political and economic philosophies seeking to shape, if not mould, the future.

The point I am making is that the report contains within it traces of these conflictual discourses which call into question, if not completely unravel, some of the apparently tightly knit threads of the argument. The language used to articulate a vision of education in the next 20 years is one which has been heavily impregnated with a technocratic and managerialist discourse. Yet, at the same time, insofar as the report also acknowledges the potential complexities and uncertainties of such a vision, it betrays an anxiety about its own conditions of possibility. Confidently assertive propositions are qualified in some instances by subordinate clauses or alternative scenarios which have the force of undermining or problematising what had previously been taken for granted. For example, after declaring that we are now living in a society which is 'essentially scientifically and technologically based' (5.26), the report goes on to express anxieties about the extent to which the pursuit of knowledge (as well as the development of skills) is likely to translate into 'applications' which may benefit society in a direct and accessible manner. For, having articulated the need to develop in individuals a series of attributes, skills and capabilities, the report concedes: 'It is also a hallmark of a civilised society that it pursues knowledge at the highest levels for its own sake and that it seeks knowledge for altruistic, and not only commercial, aims' (5.44). In other words, there is acknowledgement here that so-called 'pure' research may also have a place in a society whose interests are larger than commercial gain. I would go further by suggesting that the question of the 'usefulness' and 'relevance' of research is unanswerable in strictly instrumental terms. From recent experience we know that much research in the mathematical and physical sciences which was deemed 'pure' has been shown to have had major applications in helping us to understand the nature of our universe as well as in practical and commercial terms (see, for example, Kaku 1998 on quantum theory).

Ultimately, then, the context which is helping to inform a changing vision of society is one which can be called into question. That is not to say, however, that the viewpoints expressed or the recommendations proposed in the Dearing Report are fundamentally flawed. In fact much of it appears to be sound – that HEIs make a contribution to the society of which they are a part, that individuals be given learning opportunities throughout life, that institutions reflect on and change organisational structures and schedules so as to facilitate greater access and respond to the diverse needs of the 'new' student body. The problems relate to the extent to which it is possible and/or desirable to treat HEIs as commercial enterprises, i.e. as sites for the production and consumption of knowledge and skills. If universities are to retain their 'distinctive continuing role ... as independent questioning institutions unconstrained by any particular political or commercial agenda' (5.23), how are they to achieve this in a society driven by commercial interests? It would be naive to suggest that the UK simply ignore global trends and competition and go its own way. This is clearly not an option in a global economy. Yet now, more than ever, there seems to be a need for reflection as well as action and for careful planning and evaluation rather than quick and easy solutions to long-term problems. Research funding and the basis on which it is determined is a case in point: there is great potential for conflict between the desire to capitalise on investment and the need to be open to research paths which are unlikely to yield immediate dividends.

OF MEANS AND ENDS

And so we have come full circle with respect to the issues that I raised at the beginning of this chapter through reference to de Bono's ideas about business and the academy, about prospective and retrospective thinking, and about the types of skills and qualities needed to design the future. While commercial, intellectual and social goals need not conflict, there is certainly room for serious disagreement over means and ends. De Bono's experience of academia has led him to value the reception which the business world has given to his ideas and to conclude that academics must adopt a new way of thinking about the world. The Dearing Report, as I have shown, also betrays a sense of unease about potential areas of conflict between, for example, the world of applied knowledge and commercial advantage and that of 'pure', disinterested but ultimately valuable research. It is a kind of clash of cultures. In my view 'shaking up academia' and demanding that HEIs justify their existence is not necessarily a bad thing. De Bono may have a point when he refers to HE in the UK as 'self-satisfied and change-resistant' (Milnes 2000: 10). Because education is an investment in the future, it is only right and proper that we take stock and examine the aims and purposes, the costs and benefits of institutions of learning in and for the twenty-first century. To consider participation rates and issues of equity and social responsibility in relation to the educational system is, likewise, no bad thing. The difficulties lie, however, in determining the best means of achieving these aims and in trying to avoid the temptation to reduce complex issues to simplistic propositions. In this, and indeed many other senses, 'communication' is key. Yet just what is meant by 'communication' is not as 'transparent' as it might appear. The question of what constitutes 'effective' communication, for example, is answerable only in relation to context – a 'good' business presentation is likely to be rather different from a 'good' research paper. In other words, as with the concepts of 'change', 'adaptability' and 'flexibility', what is meant in practice, as well as in theory, cannot be taken for granted. It is this 'taken-for-grantedness' that I would like to challenge in subsequent chapters, with particular reference to the hidden assumptions that underlie the notion of key skills and employability and by looking at 'theories' of language learning and usage which take issue with the notion of transparency.

2
Key skills and employability

TERMINOLOGICAL ISSUES

While noting that the needs of employers are complex and not easily defined, a joint CVCP/DfEE report, issued in November 1998, lays out those sets of skills which, according to its research, the majority of employers feel to be necessary in the workplace. These so-called employability skills include traditional intellectual skills, the 'new' core or key skills, personal attributes and knowledge about how organisations work. The report lists under each major category the kind of skills and attributes that it has in mind. So, for example, the traditional intellectual skills include critical evaluation of evidence and the ability to argue logically, apply theory to practice, model problems qualitatively and quantitatively, and to challenge taken-for-granted

assumptions. The 'new' core or key skills enumerated are communication, application of number, information and communications technology, improving one's own performance and working with others. While it is helpful to have an indication of the types of skills which employers recognise as key, problems of definition and indeed of implementation still remain. Terms such as 'critical evaluation of evidence' and 'the ability to argue logically' may appear transparent but, as we know, appearances can be deceptive.

The problem is that many of the concepts to which these 'skills' are attached or in which they are embedded do not equate neatly to a predetermined set of teachable outcomes. The desire to make explicit the kinds of processes, functions, skills and outcomes which take place in HE programmes may be a laudable one insofar as it represents an attempt to be inclusive rather than exclusive. It is, however, a very difficult and complex task, which requires both (insider) knowledge and the ability to communicate that knowledge in an accessible but non-trivial way. The danger of listing skills and attributes in a largely decontextualised and categorical manner is that it obscures the cultural and contextual factors which help to support and ultimately shape their development.

In other words, critical evaluation of evidence and the ability to argue logically are conceptual constructs and analytical tools rather than merely instrumental and transferable skills. Thus to present them as generalised and decontextualised skills is to render them virtually meaningless. Devoid of the context which informs and shapes their acquisition, they become 'content-free' zones. In reality, what constitutes 'evidence' in law, for example, may be rather different to what constitutes 'evidence' in literature or in sociology, while the notion of critical evaluation is likely to relate not only to discipline but also to perspective. Even groups of like-minded professionals do not always agree on what constitutes a 'good' critical evaluation (of the

evidence). Evidence is used to make a case, to help support a point of view. It is not used indiscriminately but rather in a selective and focused manner as part of a larger agenda. I am not suggesting that professionals, including academics, skew evidence to suit. Rather I am pointing out that perspectives and points of view help to focus the way in which evidence is marshalled and arguments are constructed. Indeed there is evidence to suggest that the ability to argue logically may not only be subject-specific (maths vs. English lit.) but also vary from culture to culture (see, for example, Connor and Kaplan 1987; Belcher and Braine 1995; Johns 1997). It may be that employers in the UK are looking for a certain kind of logic, a particularly Western way of approaching information and situations, but this is neither obvious nor problem-free given both the increasingly global nature of enterprises and the shifts in student and professional populations. My point is that in the absence of contextual and cultural factors, what these skills actually mean (and how one might set about inducing their development) is far from self-evident.

TEXT AND CONTEXT

As I have indicated in the preceding chapter, I am not in principle against HEIs being responsive to societal needs, nor indeed to them being required to reflect on their role and justify their existence. My concern, rather, is that the influences currently acting on HEIs may be too heavily weighted in favour of economic rather than intellectual and (long-term) social arguments. It is one thing to note the importance of HEIs in the production of graduates attractive to employers and citizens likely to be able to contribute to the wellbeing of the nation. It is quite another to gear the entire HE system to the economic needs of the country. Even if, for the sake of argument, concession were to be made to the primacy of economic factors, a number of problems would

still remain. I have touched on one of them already: that is, the assumption that 'explicitness' and enumeration of skills and attributes are the key to a series of successful learning outcomes.

To be fair, in considering the issue of 'stand-alone' versus 'embedded' approaches to the delivery of employability skills, there is some recognition in the report of the complexity and scope of the problem and of the need to weigh up short-term, less costly 'fixes' against long-term and (almost invariably) more expensive solutions. Yet even here the arguments are primarily pragmatic and strategic rather than intellectual or philosophic. There is, unlike in the Dearing Report, no discussion of the *social significance* of such moves nor any *critical enquiry* into the plausibility of developing curricula which explicitly set out to deliver a series of (pre-identified) skills and attributes. There appears to be an assumption of a one-to-one correspondence between the acquisition of knowledge, the development of particular skills and attributes, and success in the workplace. The idea that the acquisition of skills may be a *by-product* of the (systematic) study of a discipline or field of study is given no voice nor are the (qualitative) differences between the world of work and the academy fully explored except insofar as there is an implicit assumption that the academy has failed/is failing to serve the world of work as well as it might. From the information contained in the Dearing Report, it would appear that there is among employers general dissatisfaction with the skills' levels of employees and indeed 25 per cent claim to wish to see 'better' communication skills among graduates. Just what they mean by 'better' communication skills is, however, not made explicit. Is it the inability of graduates to effect a smooth transition to the different (communicational) demands of the world of work that is at issue here or are we talking about the 'mechanics' of language such as spelling, punctuation and basic syntax? Is the problem one of oral or of written communication or both?

THE CHANGING COMMUNICATIONAL LANDSCAPE

Given that the communicational landscape is changing fast under the influence of communications technology, the primacy of the printed text or document can no longer be taken for granted in the twenty-first century. Indeed, according to Kress, we have entered an age when visual literacy will predominate and when the multi-modal features of text will increasingly come to the fore (Kress 2000a). In such a shifting communicational landscape, there is bound to be the occasional mismatch between knowledge and know-how. That is not to say that HEIs should ignore the impact of new technology on modes of communication and continue to approach the production of meaning in the same way. On the contrary, it is precisely the role of HEIs to research the effects of new technology on the production and dissemination of meaning. Employers indeed stand to benefit from an informed understanding of the communicational potential (and limitations) of the various modes and media. Already questions are being raised, both by academics and by employers, regarding the effects – cultural, institutional, textual and interactional – of the use of e-mail in organisations. The point is that the social impact of scientific and technological advances may not always be immediately apparent. What appears to be simply a (more or less neutral) communicational tool is turning out to have all sorts of unforeseen consequences, both positive and negative. It is precisely in such areas, in enabling 'society to make progress through an understanding of itself and its world' (Dearing 1997: 5.10) that HE has a crucial role to play.

Insofar, therefore, as partnership between industry and the academy might lead to greater understanding of their different (and complementary) roles, there is much to be gained by it. The Dearing Report speaks of 'an implicit compact between higher education and the world of work, based on how much each has to offer the other and

the potential advantage in realising the mutual gain' (1.24). In other words, where their interests coincide or complement one another, it may be sensible to ensure a measure of mutual co-operation. Dialogue between employers and HEIs may help to close the perceived skills gap as academic institutions come to understand better the demands placed on students in a changing world of work and employers realise the value of a well-educated (rather than merely well-trained) workforce. There are, however, still likely to be tensions between HEIs and the world of work where their goals do not overlap. This, it seems to me, is as it should be. For, as the Dearing Report points out, 'higher education should see itself as having a distinctive responsibility to act as the conscience of the nation' (5.40). Rather than being simply a training school for the world of work, HEIs need to retain the kind of distinctive role that could be compromised by over-emphasis on commercial or narrowly pragmatic objectives.

MANAGING CHANGE

A publication which tries to address some of the complexities of the key skills debate in a constructive manner is that produced by Drummond et al. (1999) with support from the Fund for the Development of Teaching and Learning. Entitled *Managing Curriculum Change in Higher Education*, it signals the fact that what is essentially at issue here is changing the culture and mode of delivery at many institutions of HE. The publication argues that successful key skills development 'is only likely to occur within a holistic and effectively managed change programme' (1.7). It concedes that 'such a programme must move beyond concerning itself with the technicalities of key skills development and also address the broader cultural and contextual factors which underpin both good practice and the change processes needed to achieve this' (1.7). There are two points of interest here: one is the acknowledgement of the fact that 'key skills provision is an extremely challenging task which requires profound and wide-ranging changes to established structures, attitudes and practice' (2.2). The second is the reference to the 'broader cultural and contextual factors' (1.7) that underpin change. Skills development needs not just to be written into the curriculum. For such an agenda to be effective, it requires a change in 'structures, attitudes and practice' which 'typically have to be promoted in a context of scarce resources and competing pressures which makes positive development difficult' (2.2).

SKILLS FOR ALL

In a still more recent DfEE publication, *Skills for All: Proposals for a National Skills Agenda* (2000), the social and economic impetus driving change is made yet more explicit. Throughout the publication there is a linkage of social and economic goals and an acknowledgement that 'lack of a specific strategy for work-related skills has been a gap in UK policy' (1.10). Although concession is initially made to 'the danger of an artificial polarisation between training and education, and of the pressure for *isolating competence from underpinning knowledge and understanding, and from the wider cultural benefits which come from learning*' (1.3 – the italics are mine), the proposals in the body of the text seem to be driven primarily by a perceived skills gap – the need to match supply and demand – as well as by a deficiency in skills. According to this publication, 'seven million adults in Britain – one in five – are functionally illiterate' (2.13), while 40 per cent of employers who participated in an employer survey felt that 'they would need higher levels of literacy and numeracy skills in their workforce' (2.14), if they were to improve their product or service.

One could of course query these data and seek a determination of, for example, what is meant in this context by 'functional illiteracy', a term which remains undefined. What seems to me to be more pertinent is the blatant way in which economic factors seem to be driving educational and social agendas. In addition the explicit linkage of skills levels and productivity reduces to a mathematical equation a complex set of social questions. It would be useful to have more information on which groups within society are 'functionally illiterate' and to seek to understand why this might be so. It may be that among these adults there are those who are literate in their own languages and cultures but who experience some difficulties in English. This is a different situation to that of the adult who has left school in Britain unable to read or write and perhaps hides another set of social and cultural factors impacting upon achievement. It is the failure of the skills agenda to engage with social and educational aspirations and failures in a wider sense rather than in a narrowly economic one that I would take issue with. In addition, the focus on skills has the effect of turning complex social and educational processes into a series of checklists of skills to be acquired without regard either for what is involved in the process or for the (contextual) relationship between process and product. The discourse discloses its own ultimately economic goals through a language which stresses productivity, efficiency, accuracy, and competence rather than, for example, (self-) fulfilment, social integration and quality of experience. It is a quantitative rather than a qualitative agenda.

THE PROCESS OF COMMUNICATION

In other words, there is a lot more here than meets the eye; there is nothing neutral about key skills. Their development is likely to require substantial organisational and curricular changes. They are far from being an 'add-on' to existing curricula but appear to go right to the heart of the learning process and the design and delivery of courses and programmes. Clearly, questions of effective implementation cannot be divorced from discussions of political and institutional agendas. In a way this serves as an illustration of my earlier point about the difficulty, if not impossibility, of separating propositions or proposals from the contexts which motivate and inform them. Language usage and the production of meaning are far from being transparent and unproblematic. The meanings we attach to linguistic items are culturally bound in the broadest sense. Cultural and contextual factors underpin our understanding of the world and the (competing) sets of discourses that circulate within it. The communicational process is one which does not fit neatly into decontextualised boxes and categories but needs to be discussed in relation to specific contexts and purposes. These are some of the issues that I would like to explore further in the next chapter in relation to 'theories' of language and learning and what it means to communicate information and ideas – in short, to make meaning – in a variety of institutional and situational contexts.

3
Theories of language and language learning

In looking closely at the discourse of the Dearing Report I have tried to draw attention to the 'mixed messages' being sent or, more accurately perhaps, I have pinpointed through analysis of the language and structures the conflicting agendas and competing interests at work. I have insisted on the contextual factors which need to be accounted for in a reading and interpretation of text and have suggested that there is more to 'communication skills' than meets the eye. The communicational process, and the 'skills' needed to engage in it, cannot be separated from the specific contexts and cultures in which the interaction takes place if one accepts that language is not an autonomous system with 'ready-made' meanings applicable to all occasions and all situations. I have indicated that concepts such as 'flexibility', 'adaptability', 'transparency' and 'explicitness' are not self-evident terms which carry unambiguous and neutral meanings but that their interpretation depends on a range of textual and contextual factors.

One of the difficulties in discussing the workings of language and the production of meaning(s) is that there is a 'common-sense' notion of communication which is sometimes at odds with both research findings and indeed 'theories' of language and learning. Whereas most people would shy away from engagement in a discussion of particle physics or quantum mechanics without specialist knowledge, 'communication' is an area where the views of non-specialists appear to carry as much weight, if not more so, than those of specialists. When, for example, employers request 'better' communication skills from their employees, there is in many instances no real appreciation of the complexities of the communicational process. It is so often taken for granted that an ability to speak or write 'effectively' depends on little other than an ability to construct sentences and to spell and punctuate 'correctly'. In a 'time equals money' culture, there is little tolerance of those who argue that producing meanings is a complicated, laborious and culturally dependent process. However, to fail to take account of accumulated knowledge about and research into language, literacy and the production of meaning(s) is to adopt a peculiarly philistine and programmatic approach which is likely to undermine the very purposes it is setting out to achieve. As indicated, what precisely employers mean by 'better' communication skills is left unanswered. One can only assume that they might be referring either to (some) graduates' inability to communicate ('effectively') in specific contexts and in a variety of modes and media to which perhaps they had not previously been exposed or that their 'style' of writing is 'inappropriate' to the communicational demands of the situation. It is somehow difficult to believe that, in an age of grammar and spell checks, 'correctness' is the main problem. There must, therefore, be other issues at stake.

It seems to me that part of the problem lies in a misunderstanding of the nature and role of language in the communicational process. As a former EAP (English for Academic Purposes) tutor who worked closely with international students preparing to enter degree-level programmes in a variety of disciplines, it became apparent that writing, reading, speaking (and listening) in an academic context required more than simply a knowledge of the English language. Rather it involved, among other things, an ability to meet the generic and discoursal expectations of disciplinary subject tutors. In a small-scale, qualitative and longitudinal study of the process of academic and disciplinary enculturation among a group of non-native speakers of English, I examined some of the factors, based on data collection and analysis, which seemed to be impacting on students' 'success' (or otherwise) at undergraduate level. I concluded that while a 'threshold level' of (English) language is a necessary condition, it is nevertheless not a sufficient one for success in academic writing. In my current capacity as Lecturer in Education with Special Reference to Academic Literacy, I am once again encountering, both research-wise and as a tutor, the inadequacies of a view which holds that 'good' writing depends on grammar and spelling. For as Creme and Lea, among other researchers and practitioners in the field have pointed out: 'writing involves much more than a working knowledge of the formal structures of written English' (Creme and Lea 1997: 2). Just what is involved in the production of meaning within particular contexts using various media is in fact an increasingly well researched area. There is, it would seem, a mismatch between what researchers or practitioners in the field have to say and the 'common-sense' view of those who see language as a (neutral) tool in the service of (more or less) clear communicational ends. According to this latter view, a sufficient grasp of the English language is all it takes to successfully communicate a given message. The fact that in reality language is used in social settings to fulfil a variety of functions is 'factored out' in the quest for teachable outcomes and transferable communicational skills.

THE MYTH OF TRANSPARENCY

The call for 'transparency', 'clarity' and, 'explicitness' in conveying ideas and information in oral or written form is evidence of a lack of understanding of the process by which meanings are produced in various (social and disciplinary) contexts. Indeed it goes against the grain of ideas about language and language usage as articulated by a range of (socio-)linguists, semioticians, philosophers of language, (socio-cognitive) psychologists and educationalists both here and abroad in the last 40 to 50 years.

It is not, however, just philosophers and researchers who have problematised language usage and the construction of meaning. Practitioners, reflecting on the experiences of student writers, have also been laying bare the assumptions hidden in calls for 'transparency' and 'explicitness' in relation to language. In a recent volume of essays entitled *Students Writing in the University*, one of the contributors and co-editors, Joan Turner, addresses the question of 'Academic literacy and the discourse of transparency'. As Turner puts it: 'In constructing language as "transparent", it has effectively denied its workings' (Turner 1999: 149). 'Academic thinking', she continues, 'tied up with notions of rationality and logic, assumes the possibility of absolute clarity of representation of knowledge' (151). It is perhaps not by chance that post-structuralist positions that point to the (ultimately) impenetrable nature of language and the irrecoverability of meaning, in an absolute sense, have found little favour in a culture which continues, by and large, to operate as if meanings carried through language were clear and unambiguous. Language has tended to be seen as a vehicle of communication which individuals or groups of individuals use to convey a (pre-meditated) message. The clarity of the message, it is assumed, depends on the sender's ability to construct his or her meaning through (more or less 'effective') use of the linguistic system. Such a view not only overlooks a number of (con)textual factors such as communicational form, purpose and relationship between the parties involved in the process; it also excludes or 'writes out' notions of rhetorical and cultural preference (see Turner 1999: 154-5). Ultimately, for Turner, it is the role of academic literacy to foreground 'the visibility of language' and to cut through 'the transparency conceptualisation' (158) by drawing attention to the 'process of shaping language and of recognising shapes in language in academic discourse' (158). Such a view posits 'a critical rather than a remedial role' (158) for academic literacy in higher education.

FROM SPEECH TO WRITING

While Turner's critique of the view of language as transparent is anchored in research and practice as it relates primarily to writing in academic contexts, Kress's book, *Learning to Write*, is essentially concerned with young children as they grapple with the difficult process of moving from speech to written text. His views accord with those already expressed which see writing, in particular, as something involving 'much more than learning the mechanics of writing' (Kress 1982: 60). For Kress, learning to write 'involves the learning of new forms of syntactic and textual structure, new genres, new ways of relating to unknown addressees' (60). Given that speech and writing are essentially different modes with different possibilities and limitations, the process of moving from speech to writing is for children (as indeed it can be for many adults) neither natural nor obvious. What is at stake, Kress maintains, 'is the overt, conscious mastery of a symbolic system' (142). It is not simply a question of transcribing speech or representing through marks on a page a (linear) sequence of ideas and information as they come to mind. Rather writing requires a conscious effort to organise ideas and information in line with purpose, (anticipated) audience, and (more or less) conventionalised textual forms or genres. It is likely, therefore, to be the product of painstaking effort and conscious deliberation rather than a spontaneous stream of conjoined ideas. For 'writing is the domain of circumspection, of (self-) censorship, reworking, editing. The development of the topic in writing is by another order: not by sequence but by hierarchy' (Kress 1982: 28).

WRITING AND CULTURE

Of course for writers for whom English is a second or additional language and who may already be competent writers in their own language(s), the challenges posed by the process of learning to write in a different textual and linguistic form within a different cultural and, perhaps, disciplinary context, are great and various. There is a body of literature in contrastive analysis and genre studies in particular which points to the culturally-specific nature of preferred modes of textual organisation and the values which attach to such 'conventionalised' or 'naturalised' modes. This appears to be the case not only for different languages but also for different disciplines. Ann Johns, for example, points out that while many scientists view texts by students of English as lacking in rigour, the latter tend to regard scientific papers as badly written and lacking in originality and imagination (Johns 1997).

Across cultures, as well as across disciplines, there are also differences in conventions in reading and writing. Broadly speaking, Japanese writers, for example, credit their readers with the ability to make connections which may remain (textually) implicit, while British writers are encouraged to be as explicit and 'reader-friendly' as possible. Indeed different languages have different expressive possibilities which do not neatly overlap. We know from the theory and practice of translation that texts in one language are *qualitatively different* from the 'same' texts in another, given the (ultimate) inseparability of form and content (see Steiner 1992). As Kress puts it, in a different context:

'The match between intended meaning and its expressibility in a language is never guaranteed. It is a happy coincidence when it comes about, but frequently it does not' (Kress 1982: 5). In other words, 'translating' thoughts into words is a highly problematic and cognitively demanding activity which, far from taking place in a vacuum, is circumscribed by cultural preferences and conventionalised norms. In such a context the notion of 'creativity' assumes a different set of meanings from those which may traditionally have been held. All writing, whether in the form of narrative or factual report, is then potentially creative insofar as the writer is using a set of representational resources to make meaning in a particular context. That meaning is not 'ready-made' but must be (re-)presented in a form appropriate to the context and purpose as determined by the set(s) of participants in the interaction.

WRITING AS MEANING-MAKING

Kress's view of language as one (of many) meaning-making resource(s) helps to shift the debate about communication away from a 'deficit model', i.e., that the writer is somehow deficient, towards a recognition of the complexities of language use and of the different 'grammars' and 'logics' that underlie different modes of communication. To focus on what is present (rather than on what is absent) and on what is 'right' (rather than on what is 'wrong') is to credit the child or learner with an attempt to make meaning.

This emphasis on meaning-making helps to redress the balance insofar as such a view places the learner at the centre rather than on the periphery of the educational process. In recognising the contextual factors which inform learning and which help to shape perceptions and capabilities, Kress is usefully focusing attention on the inherent difficulties of learning to write and pointing to the failures of a system which has misrepresented the production of (written) language. 'Linguists and teachers', he writes, 'naturally attempt to represent the relationship [between sounds and letters] as a basically logical one – as many different reading schemes and sounding/spelling rules demonstrate. But this attempt makes the child's position worse: a system which is largely arbitrary is presented as basically logical, the child is invited to grasp the (non-existent) logic of the system, and when he fails his inadequacies are clearly apparent and confirmed' (Kress 1982: 180).

Such an attempt to systematise and characterise as 'natural' and 'logical' relationships that are cultural, conventional and contextual continues throughout the educational system so that it is little wonder that things go awry. Students who leave university unable to communicate effectively, according to employers, may well have been able to produce essays which sufficiently conformed to tutor expectations that they passed the course and were awarded their degrees. If they are unable to 'transfer' their written communication skills, it may not be due to personal inadequacies or declining standards but rather a misapprehension with respect to the role of language in successful communication. In other words, to be able to perform well in one area does not guarantee success in another, nor does ability to write well or meaningfully in one context for a particular type of audience guarantee success in all communicative contexts irrespective of audience. The company executive most likely has different communicational forms and requirements to that of the fashion designer or media personality. Language will be differently inflected and realised in forms typical of the functions and requirements of the particular context and medium. Acquiring conventionalised, cultural forms and behaviours is not a direct function of ability to use the English language. Successful interaction and communication depend rather on a range of contextual and cultural factors.

WRITING AND CREATIVITY

Such a view also calls into question notions of creativity. Insofar as every text is characterised by difference and is the product of a particular set of interests and motivation, all writing or 'making' can, according to Kress, be viewed as creative. What makes the difference is the individual's access to and (conscious) mastery of (a range of) representational resources. When employers speak of creativity or creative thinking, it is not always clear exactly what they have in mind. When, in the Dearing Report, mention is made of ' creativity' and 'design' as capabilities or qualities which 'matter at least as much as the content of knowledge' (4.32), there is clearly an attempt to place value on these concepts. What is less clear is what is meant by these terms. Insofar as concern is articulated that disciplines as currently constituted may block 'flexibility of thinking' (cf. 4.31), which may or may not be the same as 'creativity', there is recognition of the sometimes 'parochial' attitudes of academics (cf. Geertz's notion of intellectual villages (Geertz 1983: 161 as quoted in Prior 1991)). As Dearing explicitly states: 'The prevailing classification of disciplines could serve the UK poorly if it inhibits the development of new programmes of study and if it means that research is focused on areas which are, in economic terms, of limited currency' (4.31). The message seems to be that rigid division of subject knowledge into disciplinary areas is likely to hinder innovation and programme design and that indeed some traditional disciplinary configurations and areas of research may prove 'of limited currency'.

One of the problems, it seems to me, with notions of creativity and innovation is that they are assumed to be self-evident and positive. There is little discussion of the potential for tension or conflict between conformity to social and institutional norms and values and (individual) attempts to 'step outside' of or criticise these norms and values. What are creativity and innovation if not an alternative way of conceiving or producing or expressing ideas and what if, as is likely, such notions come into conflict with received opinion? What facilitative mechanisms will there be socially and institutionally to enable 'creative' or 'divergent' thinking? And if the university is to be more than a service industry, what guarantees can there be in terms of liberty to think beyond agendas set by government or business or the consumer society? If 'creativity' comes with strings attached and 'innovation' means anything useful to the economy, then perhaps we should simply dispense with the pretence of doing anything other than meeting a (particular) economic and political agenda. A recent article in the *Times Higher Educational Supplement* (*THES*) points to the dangers for society when academics fail to speak out against the dominant economic interests funding their research and curtailing their creativity. If researchers' renewal of contracts and continued funding depend on their agreeing to release results at the bidding of funding bodies and policy units rather than in the light of public interest, then the likelihood is that 'innovative' science will be shaped by political and economic rather than by scientific or social interests. As the article concludes: 'The case of BSE shows only too clearly that the public interest is not at all the same as the generation of wealth and making ourselves useful to policy-makers' (THES: 3 November 2000).

LANGUAGE AND SOCIETY

It should by now be evident that embedded as it is in a social context, language, far from being transparent, carries with it traces of the debates and perspectives which inform it. Communicational interactions are shaped as much by context as by language. Audience, purpose, generic conventions and disciplinary interests motivate the shaping and interpretation of text. For Kress, the individual user of the representational resources of the language has the potential, given his or her disposition and interest, to make (new) meaning(s). Clearly the representational resources to which an individual has access is a product of social and cultural factors. Students coming from other language backgrounds and educational systems must learn the expressive potentialities and limitations of what, for them, is a different social, cultural and linguistic system. There is nothing 'natural' about 'English' modes of communication. Ways of writing or expressing meaning can come to seem natural or extraordinarily well suited to their purpose and it can be difficult to separate one's sense of self from particular modes of expression. The research which has been conducted on language and identity, as well as language and gender (see Clark and Ivanic 1997), would support the view that modes of expression are far from neutral but relate to social and political structures, hierarchies and power. Indeed for some, having to adopt another's language (and culture and way of thinking) amounts to a kind of violation or abnegation of self. What may be articulated, in what context and in what form is 'regulated' to a greater or lesser extent by social, institutional and disciplinary norms (see Foucault 1971). Penalties are imposed on those who fail to conform to these norms. Yet, at the same time, it is precisely the ability to produce alternative views and invent new forms, meanings and ideas that underlies the possibility of change and progress. If we accept that language and thought are closely implicated or related, then *what cannot be articulated cannot be realised* (in both senses of the word).

LANGUAGE AND THOUGHT

The role of language in conceiving, articulating and realising ideas is, then, far from being a trivial or a mechanical one. Indeed, as Vygotsky (1962) makes clear, language is a cognitive tool instrumental in the articulation and development of thought. To make meaning is to engage in a cognitive act Kress 2000a: 156, a cognitive act which has a double root insofar as meaning 'belongs in the realm of language as much as in the realm of thought' (5). By this, Vygotsky appears to be recognising the fact that the linguistic system precedes the individual utterances of particular users; words have a history and conventional usage. While the individual user is at liberty in context to extend the range of possible meanings, s/he is unable to 'remove' or 'efface' entirely the (conventionalised) meaning-intention. (The fact, for example, that 'wicked' is used by particular groups of young people to mean 'great' does not of necessity entail a permanent change in the dictionary definition of wicked, although corpus-based dictionaries would of course register and thereby, to a certain extent, legitimise its usage.) For Vygotsky 'man's thought reflects conceptualized actuality' (7). 'A word does not refer to a single object but to a group or to a class of objects. Each word is therefore already a generalization' (5). It is as if a word has a schematic structure that is realised in particular contexts according to the design and purpose of the user of the language. At the same time (individual) language use is constrained by social, linguistic and cultural factors. According to Vygotsky, 'the word maintains its guiding function in the formation of genuine concepts' (81). Words influence thought and thought in turn is determined by language, i.e., 'by the linguistic tools of thought and by the sociocultural experience of the child' (51).

Given that language is an aid to thought – a kind of conceptual tool – it follows that access to forms of language is tantamount to access to modes of cognition. A word, however, is not a static object to be acquired and used unconsciously. Rather 'word meanings are dynamic … formations' (Vygotsky 1962: 124); words are produced in and relate to specific contexts which frame their meaning. They are inflected by individual users for particular purposes in particular situations. 'To understand another's speech', writes Vygotsky, 'it is not sufficient to understand his words – we must understand his thought. But even that is not enough – we must understand its motivation' (151). On the one hand, then, 'words play a central part ... in the development of thought' (153), while on the other hand, and at the same time, words reflect 'human consciousness' (153). The production of meaning is a dynamic process, 'a continual movement back and forth from thought to word and from word to thought' (125).

CONCLUDING REMARKS

The kind of views expressed by practitioners, theorists, and researchers in the field, that language is far from transparent (see Turner 1999: 149 ff.), that meanings are made from available representational resources in social contexts by individual users for particular purposes (cf. Kress 2000a: 152 ff.) and that the relationship between language and thought is infinitely complex and dynamic (cf. Vygotsky 1962) certainly go against the grain of the 'popular' view of language as a vehicle of communication. They problematise the communicational process and highlight the need for a critical view of language. Yet to see language as problematic rather than as a skill to be acquired is exactly what the policy documents, employers, and economic interests are failing to take on board. To treat language as a serious object of study, to make it visible, as Turner has it, is to depart from instrumental and short-term agendas and to require intellectual, as well as economic, resources to be brought to bear on the contexts and interests which circumscribe the process of meaning-making. Such a qualitative and intellectually challenging task runs counter to the notion of writing, in particular, and communication, in general, as a set of acquirable skills which can then be readily transferred to a variety of disciplinary, institutional and societal contexts. Rather, such an approach ultimately calls into question 'ready-made' solutions, 'quick fixes' and static conceptualisations. In the final chapter I would like to reflect on the implications for teaching and learning of the perspectives outlined here and to suggest that policy pronouncements which are motivated by political and economic interests at the expense of intellectual concerns are unlikely to produce the kind of 'flexible', 'creative' and 'productive' citizens which the Dearing Report claims to be a requirement for the future well-being of the nation.

4
Implications for teaching and learning

THE CULTURE OF EXPECTATION

Central to many of the debates currently taking place in the educational arena is the notion of expectations. The Dearing Report explicitly makes reference to the fact that 'people's expectations of publicly funded services have risen and they no longer accept unquestioningly what is offered' (4.59), the assumption of course being that in the past students simply accepted what was on offer and registered no complaints about the content, delivery or objectives of the programme on which they were enrolled. Recent provision of student charters is also an indication of an underlying concern with what 'consumers' of or participants in the higher education system can expect. It is perhaps not by chance that this focus on expectations has emerged along with a review of funding arrangements. For if, as is increasingly the case, even in publicly funded institutions, many students, including international and part-time (post-graduate) students, are making substantial contributions to their own education, then not only must the quality of that education be assured but they must also expect to derive some benefit from it in professional, educational or social terms. In addition the likely consequence of the expansion of HE is that the necessarily more diverse population will be less culturally and socially homogeneous than in the past. It will be necessary not only to cater to different needs but to recognise and value diversity. Given that HE was traditionally the preserve of an elite in Britain, one of the challenges being faced by the tertiary sector today is how to negotiate difference. The academy is having to respond to social and cultural heterogeneity at a time of financial restraint and cultural relativity. As the Dearing Report acknowledges: 'In some respects, there is no longer a shared set of cultural norms or values' (4.56). Widening participation, access, and equal opportunities necessitate changing attitudes and values, if they are to translate from (informed) policy to (principled) practice.

The point is that the nature of the compact between HE and society is indeed in question and that the focus on expectations – what society can expect of HE and what the role of HE should be in a changing world – is a reflection of the manner in which the debate is being shaped. This is not necessarily a bad thing; it does not seem unreasonable to enquire how the contributions of tax-payers are being spent. The terms of the debate, however, are far from neutral, since they derive from a particular historical, political and economic context and set of discourses. In addition, expectations are socially and culturally constructed. Changes in society are articulated and represented. These (sometimes conflicting) representations in turn affect perceptions and understandings of what is happening on the ground. It is in this sense that the discourse of expectation not only reflects but also constitutes shifting perceptions and 'realities'.

The notion of expectations also fails to disclose the complex set of relationships and contextual factors underwriting it. 'People's expectations' begs the question of which people or groups of people and of what kind of expectations they may (or may not) share. If 'society' has a right to expect certain things of 'HE', then surely 'HE' can expect 'society' to help it meet these expectations, which presumably are subject to negotiation rather than simply being imposed. Neither society nor HE is homogeneous but each is made up of different interest groups and types of participants. Their expectations and motivations are not necessarily going to be consistent with one another. Indeed they are likely to come into conflict. The notion of 'relevant' higher education provision is a case in point: what constitutes relevance and relevant to whom? If student choice be 'the main shaper of the system' (5.52), to what extent is this consistent with the expectation that HE have a 'distinctive responsibility to act as the conscience of the nation' (5.40)?

What students can expect from institutions and what academics and administrators can expect of students is at the heart of the teaching and learning process. Again these sets of expectations are in a state of flux and are being 'worked out' in relation to contextual factors – social, economic and political. Times have changed and universities, even those with international reputations, are having to respond in some measure to demand. Cultural norms are being reshaped and redefined as different interests and constituencies brush up against one another.

STUDENT SUPPORT AND GUIDANCE

With respect to communication skills and the knowledge economy, these debates are being played out in a number of different arenas. The kind of provision, both academic and in terms of support, that students can expect from institutions is one such arena. Given the increasing diversity of the student population, a call for guidance and support of a more extensive and systematic kind, would not seem to be unreasonable. There is nothing 'natural' about academic modes of behaviour and ways of representing disciplinary and intellectual interests. On the contrary there are culturally constructed forms and genres – the seminar, the tutorial, the lecture, the term paper, the dissertation, etc. – which students are required to understand and participate in. When some of these students also come from different (academic) cultures and are operating in a language – English – which they have acquired for study and other social purposes, the question of needs and expectations as well as of culture and communication becomes increasingly pertinent. Whose language, whose culture? Communicating in which context, and by what means?

It is obvious that there are different 'takes' on these issues, but none of them is entirely 'neutral', 'objective' or 'transparent'. The focus on communication skills, for example, belies the social and cultural orders that inform and help to construct a particular communicative space. Lettered representation and particular forms of the written language tend to be privileged in the academy. Disciplinary values and what are considered to be appropriate types of knowledge are reflected in the genres and conventionalised epistemic forms realised in a variety of contexts in the academy. Yet these representational systems are not static but are open to challenge and negotiation. To be in such a position, however, requires 'insider' knowledge and a firm control of representational media, including language. It is in this sense that access to linguistic resources is crucial to success in academia. For contributions to knowledge are constituted largely through written (rather than visual) text which seeks to show familiarity with, as well as marking difference from, disciplinary discourses.

THE CONTEXT OF COMMUNICATION

The 'theories' of language which I have reviewed and which highlight the complexities and possibilities of the communicative process and the role of language in elaborating concepts, such as those by Kress and Vygotsky, are at odds with a view of language as transparent medium and skill to be acquired in decontextualised settings. By implication, 'stand-alone' courses, that is, courses which are not embedded in subject-specific contexts, are less likely to be effective than those where notions of text are firmly embedded in particular disciplinary contexts. With respect to academic literacy, then, the ideal would be to have subject-specific student groups or groups in the same field of study so that students are exposed to examples of successful pieces of course work, reports and dissertations in their area. Research has shown that what is considered to be 'good' writing or a successful dissertation in one area is not necessarily highly valued in another (Leki 1995; Johns 1997). A successful Humanities student will, for example, not necessarily be equally successful in the Social Sciences unless s/he gets to grips with the differing academic and disciplinary conventions and expectations. This would suggest that a command of English – its syntactic structures and lexis – is far from being a sufficient condition for communicating meaning. Indeed, if as Vygotsky asserts, 'meaning is an act of thought' (Vygotsky 1962: 5), then meaning is made not given. This, however, would hold equally for both writer and reader. One cannot assume that it is always the writer who is 'at fault'. In some instances it may be that a particular reader fails to follow the 'logic' of a text for reasons which may include cultural, social or ideological differences rather than 'lack of clarity' or 'lack of structure' on the part of the writer. (The resistance of much of the British academy to 'continental', especially postmodernist philosophies, is a case in point, since the premises on which they are based and the highly conceptual manner in which they are generally articulated is at odds with the British pragmatic and empirical tradition.) For what constitutes 'clarity' or a 'sense of structure' is not a universal but rather depends on context and culture. By and large, those who move across cultures, languages or disciplines are aware at first-hand of the relativity of values and the arbitrariness of conventions which can all too easily assume the character of being natural rather than naturalised. Indeed there is a body of literature pertaining to the act of reading and the making of meaning that suggests that all texts are schematic with gaps and points of indeterminacy, requiring of the reader an effort to construct rather than simply 'read off' meaning (see, for example, Iser 1978; also Wallace 1988).

In other words, meaning is not readily available and accessible to all regardless of culture, background, interest and motivation. The idea, still prevalent in some EAP courses, that access to a list of linguistic structures and functions equates to a knowledge of text and a capacity to produce meaning-in-context, is one which has severe limitations in practice. In a sense the problem relates to the relationship between form and content or procedural and substantive knowledge. While for analytic purposes we may choose to focus separately on 'what is being said' and 'how it is being articulated', in reality the 'formal' properties of text (e.g. layout, sequence, choice of lexis and of grammatical structures) are contributing to the production of meaning. Additionally, while a consciously and carefully constructed text will suggest a particular set of readings, there is no guarantee that an individual reader will 'pick up' the signals and interpret the text in the way intended by the writer. For while taken as a whole there may be a 'logic' to a particular text, a 'logic' evidenced in the text and 'recovered' by the efforts of a sympathetic and/or expert reader, it cannot be taken for granted that other readers will derive the same 'meaning'. For, ultimately, texts relate to larger structures and contexts – historical, cultural, political and social – which inform them and help to generate particular types of meaning.

WIDENING PARTICIPATION: DISCOURSE AND DIVERSITY

All of this has implications for teaching and learning in the era of mass HE. It cannot be taken for granted that all students regardless of academic, socio-economic and linguistic background will be coming to written and/or oral tasks in the same way, or that they will understand texts in similar fashion. Not only will the discourse of particular disciplines be differentially available to them depending on prior experience and enculturation but their willingness or capacity to 'adapt' to sets of conventions and expectations will in turn depend on motivation, purpose, and sense of ownership and engagement. For learning to take place in a real sense, students must feel that what they have to bring to the learning and teaching situation is being valued. At the same time they will wish to understand the 'rules of the game' and to feel that the kinds of knowledge they are gaining are productive and generative rather than reductive and (self-)limiting.

With respect to the production of meaning in academic and other communicational contexts, it is clear that a transmission and deficit model not only fails to account for the intricacies and realities of the learning process but implies a view of knowledge which is outmoded and unlikely to be productive in the twenty-first century. The diversity and extent of the new student population as well as the anticipated changes in patterns of employment and modes of social life require a re-organisation of HE at a deep rather than at a superficial level. It is not enough to provide language support to groups of international and 'non-traditional' students in ways which suggest that language can be 'separated out' from its disciplinary and cultural context. By the same token, neither is it useful to suggest that disciplinary specialists who may have little knowledge of applied language study and the production of written text be solely responsible for helping students develop as proficient writers in the field. Increasing numbers of international students, many of whom are successful products of their own educational systems, also present a challenge to institutions from a number of perspectives. At higher and more specialised levels of study, the kind of English being used may be quite unlike that which has allowed such students to communicate meaning successfully in other contexts. The expectation (or requirement) that academic texts be written in 'grammatical' English and conform to the conventionalised norms set by and for (particular) groups of native speakers in the language imposes on EAL students (students of English as an Additional Language) a matrix which is more than merely linguistic. For language, as we have seen, is embedded in particular cultural and conceptual (as well as grammatical) contexts.

I have already argued in relation to theories of language and learning that making meaning is a much more sophisticated process than the combining of grammatical and lexical elements on a page. Through analysis of written text, Kress (1994) has shown that the 'logic' of written text is different to that of spoken text in significant ways. Broadly speaking, written text may be characterised as hierarchical rather than sequential. Furthermore, there are different kinds of written text each with their 'generic' characteristics and markers which, while relatively stable, nevertheless change over time. These changes are motivated by a variety of factors which relate to societal, cultural and epistemic changes in what are sometimes quite subtle and complex ways.

It seems to me that 'adaptation' and 'communication' are a two-way rather than a one-way process. This is not to deny or override the real differences between student and lecturer in terms of expertise and power but to acknowledge that meaningful communication in the sense in which I have been using it, i.e. meaning as an act of thought on the part of reader and writer, necessarily imposes a dialogic rather than a monologic relationship. There is a danger that ways of speaking and ways of writing that relate to a particular time and place will be seen as the norm for all times and all places. The challenge for the academy in the twenty-first century will be to recognize and value diversity while trying to ensure equal access to the (still) powerful literacies. At the same time, however, it may be useful to reflect on the cultural relativity of some of our most cherished norms and to realise that the range of 'motivated conjunctions of meaning and form' (Kress and van Leeuwen 1996: 11) may be broader than that dictated by tradition or cultural preference. As a Chilean student attending a Masters writing workshop led by a colleague and myself remarked: 'It's much more than grammar. It's a view of the world'. Inscribing (and therefore constituting) a view of the world through grammatical (and other) resources is a particularly powerful form of communication privileged by academics. In a world where 50 per cent of young people are being encouraged to participate in this endeavour, it may be that forms of knowledge and modes of expression prevalent in the past come under critical enquiry and are reinscribed in the future in line with a new set of purposes and motivations. This, it seems to me, is to be welcomed rather than resisted.

REFERENCES

Belcher, D. and Braine, G. (1995) (eds), *Academic Writing in a Second Language*. New Jersey: Ablex Publishing Corporation.

de Bono, E. (2000), *The De Bono Code Book*. London: Viking.

Clark, R. and R. Ivanic (1997), *The Politics of Writing*. London: Routledge.

Connor, U and Kaplan R.B. (eds) (1987), *Writing across Languages: Analysis of 22 texts*. Reading, MA; Wokingham: Addison-Wesley.

Creme, P. and M. Lea (1997), *Writing at University: A guide for students*. Buckingham: Open University Press.

CVCP/DfEE (1998), *Skills Development in Higher Education*. London: DfEE.

Dearing Committee Report (1997), *Higher Education in the Learning Society*. London: HMSO.

DfEE (2000), *Skills for All: Proposals for a National Skills Agenda*. London: DfEE.

Drummond *et al.* (1999), *Managing Curriculum Change in Higher Education*. Sheffield: UCoSDA.

Foucault, M. (1971), *'L'Ordre du discours: Leçon inaugurale au Collège de France prononcée le 2 décembre 1970*. Paris: Gallimard; English version included in *The Archaeology of Knowledge*, trans. A. M. Sheridan Smith, London: Routledge.

Geertz, C. (1983), quoted in Prior 1991.

Iser, W. (1978), *The Act of Reading*. Baltimore and London: The Johns Hopkins University Press.

Johns, A. (1997), T*ext, Role, and Context: Developing academic literacies*. Cambridge: Cambridge University Press.

Kaku, M. (1998), *Visions*. Oxford: Oxford University Press.

Klein, N. (2000), *No Logo*. London: Flamingo.

Kress, G. (1992), *Learning to Write*. London: Routledge.

Kress, G. (2000a), 'Design and transformation: new theories of meaning'. In B. Cope and M. Kalantzis (eds), *Multiliteracies*. London and New York: Routledge.

Kress, G. (2000b), 'Multimodality'. In B. Cope and M. Kalantzis (eds), *Multiliteracies*. London and New York: Routledge.

Kress, G. and T. van Leeuwen, (1996), *Reading Images: The grammar of visual design*. London: Routledge.

Leki, I. (1995), 'Good writing: I know it when I see it'. In D. Belcher and G. Braine (eds), *Academic Writing in a Second Language*. New Jersey: Ablex Publishing Corporation.

Milnes, A. (2000), 'How I got here: "You have to design the future" '. *The Independent*, 7 September: 10.

Prior, P. (1991) 'Contextualizing writing and resonse in a graduate seminar'. *Written Communication* 8 (3): 267 – 310.

Steiner, G. (1992), *After Babel*. Oxford: Oxford University Press.

Turner, J. (1999), 'Academic literacy and the discourse of transparency'. In C. Jones, J. Turner and B. Street (eds), *Students Writing in the University*. Amsterdam: John Benjamins.

Vygotsky, L. (1962), *Thought and Language*. Cambridge, MA: MIT Press.

Wallace, C. (1988), *Learning to Read in a Multicultural Society*. London: Prentice Hall.